PUMPKIN PAINTING

PUMPKIN PAINTING

Jordan
McKinney

Sterling Publishing Co., Inc.   New York
A Sterling/Chapelle Book

FOR CHAPELLE:
Jo Packham, Owner
Cathy Sexton, Editor
Staff: Malissa Boatwright,
    Rebecca Christensen,
    Amber Hansen, Holly
    Hollingsworth, Susan
    Jorgensen, Susan Laws,
    Amanda McPeck, Barbara
    Milburn, Pat Pearson,
    Leslie Ridenour, Cindy
    Rooks, Cindy Stoeckl,
    Nancy Whitley
Designers: Renee Coles, Kathy
    Frongner, Holly Fuller,
    Sharon Ganske, Tammy
    Johnson, Jamie Pierce,
    Phillip Romero, Alison
    Timothy, Amy Williams
Kevin Dilley, Photographer
Hazen Photography

If you have any questions or
comments or would like
information on specialty
products featured in this book,
please contact Chapelle, Ltd.,
Inc., P.O. Box 9252, Ogden, UT
84409 • (801) 621-2777 •
(801) 621-2788 Fax

Library of Congress Cataloging-in-Publication Data
McKinney, Jordan.
        Pumpkin painting / by Jordan McKinney.
                p.   cm.
        "A Sterling / Chapelle book."
        Includes index.
        ISBN 0-8069-4858-2
        1. Halloween decorations. 2. Jack-o-lanterns. 3. Acrylic
painting. I. Title.
        TT900.H32M38 1996
        745.594'1--dc20   96-15594
                                                                              CIP

10 9 8 7 6 5 4 3 2 1

Published by Sterling Publishing Company, Inc.
387 Park Avenue South, New York, NY 10016
© 1996 by Chapelle Ltd.
Distributed in Canada by Sterling Publishing
c/o Canadian Manda Group, One Atlantic Avenue, Suite 105
Toronto, Ontario, Canada M6K 3E7
Distributed in Great Britain and Europe by Cassell PLC
Wellington House, 125 Strand, London WC2R 0BB, England
Distributed in Australia by Capricorn Link (Australia) Pty Ltd.
P.O. Box 6651, Baulkham Hills, Business Centre, NSW 2153, Australia
Printed in Hong Kong
All Rights Reserved

Sterling ISBN 0-8069-4858-2

TABLE OF CONTENTS

This book was created for the painting enthusiast to take the art of painting to a new dimension. The young and the old can enjoy transforming ordinary gourds into incredible works of art!

THE GOURD FAMILY

Pumpkins are part of the gourd family, as are melons and squash. Pumpkins and melons, however, are considered to be fruit, and all varieties of squash are considered vegetables.

All gourds have a thick, tough skin. Painting, carving, and embellishing can be done in the same manner on any variety.

Gourds are grown in several colors, including various shades of orange, yellow, green, brown, and white. Try picking a gourd in a color that will eventually be the background color for the chosen artwork. This will eliminate a base coat.

Because of the unusual shapes in which many gourds can be found, creativity is unlimited. Refer to photos on pages 15 and 37. Try turning a pumpkin on its side and use the stem as part of the design. Refer to photos on pages 19 and 20.

Because of the varying sizes of gourds (especially pumpkins!), the patterns provided can easily be adapted to fit any size. Once a determination has been made regarding the general size of the gourd to be used, a photo copy can be made of the pattern in either an enlarged or a reduced state.

CHOOSING THE PERFECT PUMPKIN

When using a fresh pumpkin for painting, choosing one that will suit the chosen pattern is very important. When choosing one for carving, it is important that the complexity of the design be taken into consideration. Match more difficult designs to large, smooth, and/or flat pumpkins.

Always use fresh pumpkins that are free from bruises and never purchase a pumpkin that does not have a stem. Once a stem has been broken off, the pumpkin will not last long. If a pumpkin can be chosen and picked from the vine, try to leave two to three inches of vine on the stem. This will allow the pumpkin to stay fresh longer.

Remember that once a pumpkin has been carved, its life expectancy is only two to five days.

EXTENDING THE LIFE OF THE PUMPKIN

Pumpkins are considered seasonal fruit and, therefore, fresh ones cannot be found year around. Fresh pumpkins can be stored for several months under controlled conditions. They must always be kept dry and cool, and must not be allowed to freeze. When storing pumpkins, keep space around each pumpkin so that air can circulate. Never stack them — if one should get a rotten spot, it could infect the entire pile!

In case fresh pumpkins cannot be found, the general instructions provided include tips for painting on plastic pumpkins, compressed styrofoam pumpkins, papier-mâché pumpkins, and pumpkins made from wood, as well as for painting on fresh pumpkins.

GENERAL INSTRUCTIONS FOR PUMPKIN PAINTING

The idea of painting on pumpkins is a relatively new one, and it has allowed pumpkins to be used in a new art form. Pumpkin painting should be kept simple, yet complex enough to keep imaginations busy!

PREPARING PUMPKINS FOR PAINTING

Because of the nature in which pumpkins are generally purchased, fresh pumpkins should be thoroughly washed and dried before patterns are transferred onto them.

BASE-COATING PUMPKINS

Sometimes a pumpkin will be painted with a design and the background will be left as the unpainted surface of the pumpkin. In some cases however, the pattern requires that the entire pumpkin surface be painted. Acrylic paints have been used on the projects in this book and the number of coats necessary will be determined primarily on the base-coat color being used. If available, spray paint can also be used to base-coat pumpkins.

When fresh pumpkins are being used, a paint sealer should be used on the entire pumpkin surface before acrylic paint is applied. This will help adhere the paint to the surface. If a paint sealer is not used, paint can easily chip off. Because the surfaces of plastic, compressed styrofoam, papier-mâché, and wooden pumpkins are rough and porous, a layer of paint sealer is not usually necessary.

TRANSFERRING PATTERNS ONTO PUMPKINS

The pattern must first be adapted to a size that will work with the size of pumpkin being used. A photo copy, enlarged or reduced appropriately, is the easiest way to assure the design will be in proportion to the size of the chosen pumpkin. If all the colors in the pattern are dark, a color copy may be necessary to get the line definition needed for pattern transferring.

• METHOD ONE

The pattern can be traced onto tracing paper and then transferred onto the pumpkin using graphite paper. Place the graphite paper between the pattern and the pumpkin with the graphite side facing the pumpkin. Tape the graphite paper and the pattern into position. Carefully, but firmly, trace the pattern using a pencil. Lift the corner slightly to make sure the pattern is transferring nicely. Once the design has been transferred, remove the pattern and the graphite paper.

• METHOD TWO

Make a photo copy of the pattern and cut it out. Place it on the pumpkin and tape it into position. Carefully trace around the pattern. When using a fresh pumpkin, use a dull pencil or a blunt object and press hard enough to make a slight indentation on the pumpkin's surface, but be very careful to not puncture it. Once the design has been transferred, remove the pattern.

PAINTBRUSHES & SPONGES

Paintbrushes are the most common tools used for painting pumpkins and good quality synthetic brushes work best when using acrylic paints. Sponges should be used when sponge painting and can be found in many different sizes and textures.

A variety of different sized paintbrushes are recommended — the size of the brush will depend upon the size of the pattern you are painting. Small, liner brushes are used for detailing and large, flat brushes are used for painting larger areas, such as base-coating. Flat chisel blenders, scrollers, and shaders might also come in handy, but are not mandatory.

BASIC PAINTING TECHNIQUES

Solid base-coating is done by applying two to three coats of acrylic paint. This will give the best coverage and an even look to the paint.

When base-coating with a "wash," add water to the acrylic paint to achieve a sheer color. The amount of water used will determine the intensity of the color. When applying a wash, work as quickly as possible, using long, even strokes, but do not overlap.

Sponge painting is done by loading the top of a sponge with paint. Blot the sponge on a paper towel until most of the paint has been removed. Apply the paint to the pumpkin by lightly "blotting" the sponge up and down. Work in a circular motion starting at the center of the pumpkin.

Highlighting and shading is done by dipping a flat brush in water and then removing the excess water from the brush by blotting it on a paper towel. Apply acrylic paint to the side of the flat brush and blend, staying in one track, until the paint fades evenly across the brush. The paint will fade from dark to light.

Dry brushing is done with a flat brush dipped in a small amount of acrylic paint. Remove the excess paint from the brush by working in a criss-cross motion on a paper towel. Using the same motion, lightly apply the paint to the pumpkin.

Always allow acrylic paints to dry thoroughly before applying additional coats or colors. When a quicker drying time is necessary, a blow dryer can be used to aid in drying the paint.

If mixing colors is necessary to get a perfect shade, mix a sufficient amount to complete the project. Excess paint can be stored in airtight containers.

DETAIL PAINTING & OUTLINING

The experience of the painter usually determines how the pumpkin will be detailed and outlined. Painter's with a great deal of detail painting experience most generally opt to detail paint using a liner brush. Painter's with little or no experience will want to use a fine- or medium-point permanent marker.

When using a liner brush, load in paint thinned with water. Pull the brush through the paint, turning as you go to get a fine point. Hold the brush perpendicular to the work and line the desired areas. The thickness of the line will be determined by the amount of pressure applied to the brush.

SEALING THE ARTWORK

After the artwork is complete and the paint is completely dry, it is recommended that an acrylic spray sealer be used to set the paint and protect the artwork. Either matte sealer or gloss sealer can be used depending on the look that is desired.

GENERAL INSTRUCTIONS FOR PUMPKIN CARVING

Pumpkin carving has been enjoyed for many, many years and, therefore, is briefly included in this book. Keep in mind that a painted pumpkin can also be accented with carved sections and some of the patterns provided can be used as patterns for simple carvings!

PREPARING PUMPKINS FOR CARVING

An opening in the pumpkin needs to be cut. Using a large, sharp knife, cut out the top for a lid or cut out the bottom of the pumpkin. Cut the lid out at an angle. This provides a ledge for the lid to rest on. For easy alignment, cut a "key" in the lid so that replacing the lid is simpler.

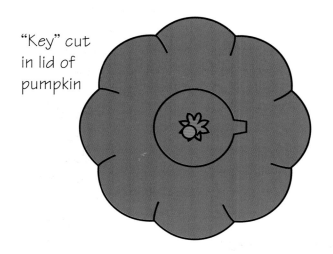

"Key" cut in lid of pumpkin

It is recommended that the lids on smaller pumpkins (less than 10" diameter) measure approximately 4" in diameter and the lids on larger pumpkins (more than 10" diameter) measure approximately 6" to 8" in diameter.

Once an opening has been cut, the seeds and the inside membrane need to be cleaned out. Scrape out the inside lining of the pumpkin until the walls are approximately 1" thick.

TOOLS NEEDED FOR PUMPKIN CARVING

Few tools are needed for carving pumpkins, but they are important. A poking tool is used for transferring patterns, a pumpkin drill is used for making holes (such as eyes), and a saw tool is used for the actual carving. A large, sharp knife is needed to cut an opening in the pumpkin and a scraping tool makes cleaning out the pumpkin cavity easier.

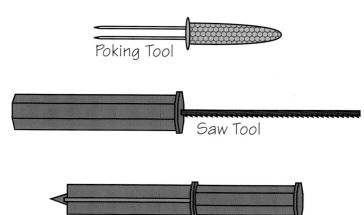

Poking Tool

Saw Tool

Pumpkin Drill

TRANSFERRING PATTERNS ONTO PUMPKINS

The pattern must first be adapted to a size that will work with the size of pumpkin being used. A photo copy, enlarged or reduced appropriately, is the easiest way to assure the design will be in proportion to the size of the pumpkin.

Transferring the pattern onto the pumpkin can be done by first aligning the design in the proper position on the surface of the pumpkin. To allow the pattern to lie snugly on the round surface of the pumpkin, make cuts from the corners of the pattern toward the center and tape it into position.

The pattern can also be pinned to the pumpkin's surface, but in order to avoid unnecessary holes on the surface, it is recommended that the pins be placed in the center of the pattern or in the grooves on the pumpkin.

Once the pattern is in position, carefully punch holes along the outside of the pattern using a poking tool. Do not attempt to poke all the way through the pumpkin, but rather just puncture the surface. For simpler designs, place the holes approximately $1/16"$ to $1/8"$ apart. If the designs are more intricate, the holes should be placed closer together. Once all the lines have been transferred, remove the pattern. If the "punched pattern" cannot easily be seen, dust the dots with flour.

DRILLING HOLES & CARVING

Before carving the design, drill holes as necessary for eyes and other small, round details using a pumpkin drill. Drilling requires pressure to be applied to the pumpkin, therefore it must be done prior to carving. If not, the drilling process could break the design in areas that have been weakened by carving.

To carve the design, use a saw tool to gently, but firmly, puncture the surface of the pumpkin. Once the saw tool has been inserted straight into the pumpkin, begin to saw from "dot to dot" at a 90° angle.

Start carving from the center of the design and work outward. Do not twist or bend the saw tool as the blade could break.

The trick to perfect carving is not being in a hurry. Once the carving is complete and all pieces are completely cut loose, use the eraser end of a pencil to gently push the carved pieces out.

If a mistake should happen, try pinning the piece back in place using toothpicks or pins.

DISPLAYING THE CARVED MASTERPIECE

Rub vegetable oil or petroleum jelly onto freshly cut areas of the pumpkin to help delay aging. If possible, carve the pumpkin the day before it is to be displayed. Place a candle inside, near the rear of the pumpkin on top of a piece of aluminum foil. When the candle is in position, carefully light it.

Cut a 1"-diameter hole in the top of the pumpkin over the candle to act as a chimney. This allows the air to circulate around the candle and will also prevent the candle from producing excess smoke. Pumpkins with smoke chimneys last longer because the heat can escape. Those that do not have chimneys will actually begin to bake from the inside out.

If no lid was cut out and the opening is in the bottom of the pumpkin, mount a candle on a cut piece of pumpkin or place one in a household candleholder or on a metal jar lid. Light the candle and then place the pumpkin over it.

If living in a climate that gets extremely cold (near freezing) at night or warmer than 60°F in the day, bring the pumpkin inside to prolong its enjoyability!

GENERAL INSTRUCTIONS FOR PUMPKIN EMBELLISHING

Pumpkin embellishing adds interest to any painted or carved pumpkin. In many cases, embellishing is the final, finishing touch that brings the creation to life. Keep in mind that embellishments can also be used on pumpkins that have not been painted or carved!

ADHESIVES USED FOR EMBELLISHING

Many types of adhesives can be used to adhere embellishments to pumpkins: glue gun and glue sticks, craft glue, and industrial-strength glue.

Hot glue is the most common adhesive used within this book, however, it can be substituted with other types of adhesive. If a pumpkin is going to be displayed out of doors where the temperature is cold, hot glue is not recommended and should be substituted with an industrial-strength glue. However, if a pumpkin is going to be displayed indoors, hot glue is a good choice.

Plastic pumpkins are manufactured with different types of plastic and in varying thicknesses. Because of this, it is recommended that hot glue not be used on plastic pumpkins. The plastic could possibly melt from the heat of the glue.

If a pumpkin has been sprayed with a product that doesn't allow adhesives to adhere properly, straight pins can be used to secure the embellishments in place.

MATERIALS USED FOR HAIR

Most pumpkins are painted or carved with a "face" and therefore lend themselves to a hair style that helps add personality and character.

Hair can be made from actual wigs and wiglets, doll hair, curly yarn, fake fur, crinkled paper-grass, fabric strips, curling ribbon, straw, wire, and polyester stuffing.

All of these choices are available in several different colors. Polyester stuffing can be spray-painted with any color!

USING CRAFT FOAM

Craft foam is available in many different colors and is a great medium for embellishing purposes. It can be cut into any shape and can easily be glued to pumpkins. If the craft foam shapes are not as secure as they need to be, straight pins can be used to help secure the pieces in place. Craft foam can be highlighted with acrylic paints. Refer to pages 15, 21, 37, and 42.

MAKING EARS AND ANTENNAE

Oftentimes, pumpkin creatures will need to be embellished with ears or antennae. Antennae can easily be made using wire or pipe cleaners and styrofoam balls or beads. Refer to pages 15, 37, and 47.

The easiest way to make ears is to cut felt fabric into triangles and simply hot-glue them into place on top of the pumpkin. Refer to pages 17 and 19.

Ears can also be made by using wire bent into any shape and size. The wire can be left uncovered or can be covered with any type of fabric by cutting the fabric to size and gluing it to the fronts and backs of the shaped wire ears. Poke the wire ends into the top of the pumpkin and shape as desired. Refer to pages 28, 33, 41, and 42.

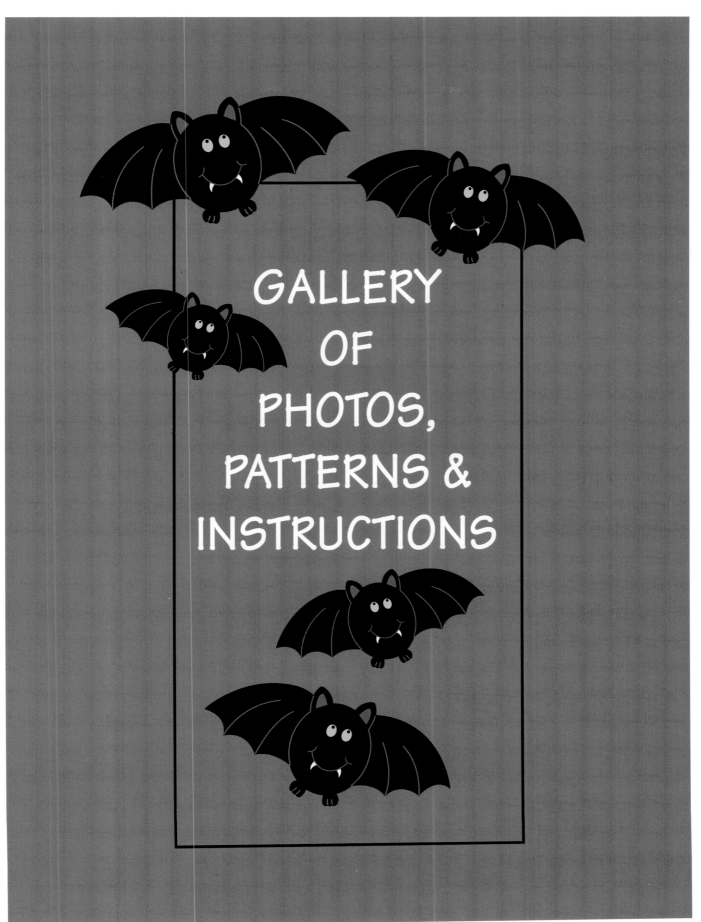

GALLERY
OF
PHOTOS,
PATTERNS &
INSTRUCTIONS

Refer to page 56

SKELETON SKULL   *Refer to page 57*

ANGRY MUMMY   *Refer to page 57*

WART WITCH   *Refer to page 58*

JAWS   *Refer to page 58*

21

Refer to page 59

Refer to page 59

SPIDER FAMILY Refer to page 61

WEB OF LIFE Refer to page 61

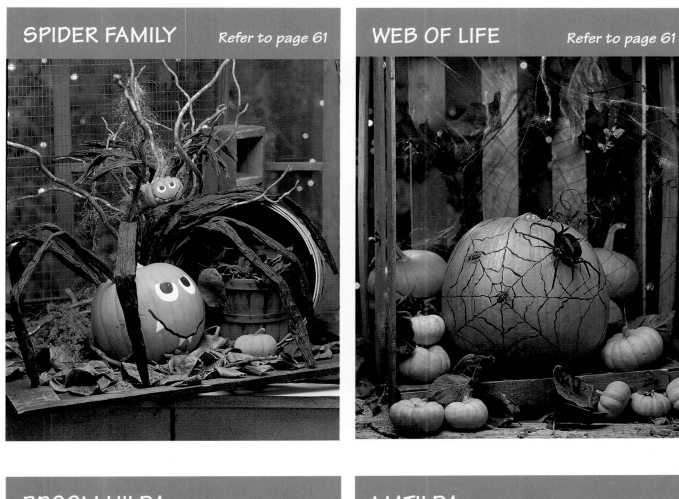

BROOM HILDA Refer to page 62

MATILDA Refer to page 62

ALLEY CAT   *Refer to page 65*

SCAR FACE   *Refer to page 65*

GRIM REAPER   *Refer to page 66*

CRESCENT MOON   *Refer to page 66*

29

CIRCUS CLOWN Refer to page 69

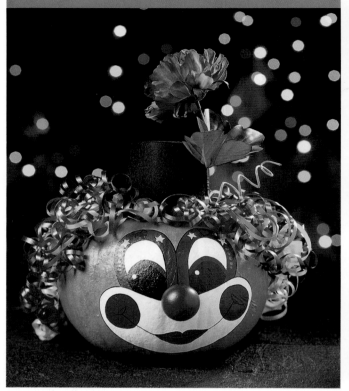

SPARKLE-EYES Refer to page 69

OH MY GOSH! Refer to page 70

FOREVER FRIENDS Refer to page 70

Refer to page 72

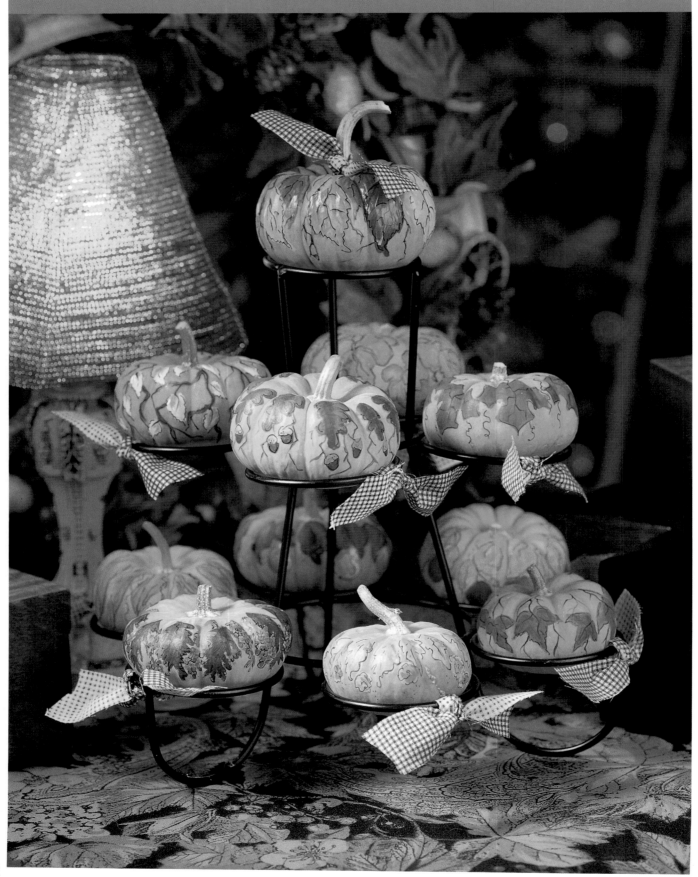

GARGOYLE
Refer to page 73

PIRATE
Refer to page 73

DEVIL
Refer to page 74

FANCY FACE
Refer to page 74

33

Refer to page 76

GOBBLING GOURD *Refer to page 77*

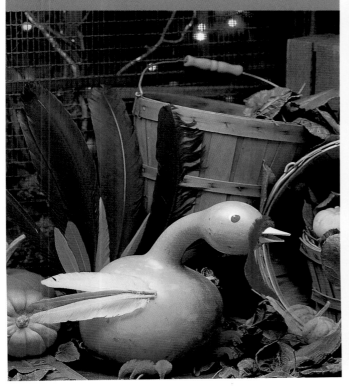

SAM SCARECROW *Refer to page 78*

Refer to page 82

Refer to page 86

FAT LADY
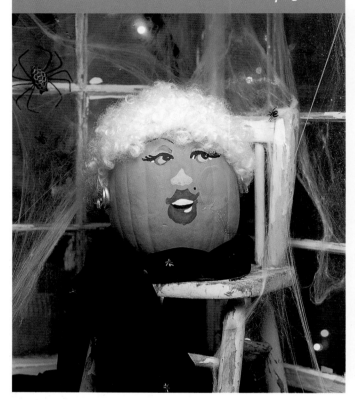
Refer to page 89

MAD SCIENTIST
Refer to page 89

BRIDE OF FRANKENSTEIN
Refer to page 90

TONGUE-LASHING CLOWN

Refer to page 90

Refer to page 91

FRANK N. STEIN & WITCH HAZEL

Pictured on page 14

Pumpkin for witch
must have a stem!

Acrylic Paints:

Black, gray, green,
moss green, sea foam
green, red, and white

Embellishment Materials:

Glue gun and glue sticks
Felt witch hat

Painting:

Paint and detail pumpkins,
referring to patterns.

Embellishing:

Carefully remove stem from top
of witch pumpkin. Hot-glue it to
front of pumpkin for a nose,
referring to pattern for placement, and hot-glue witch hat to
top of pumpkin.

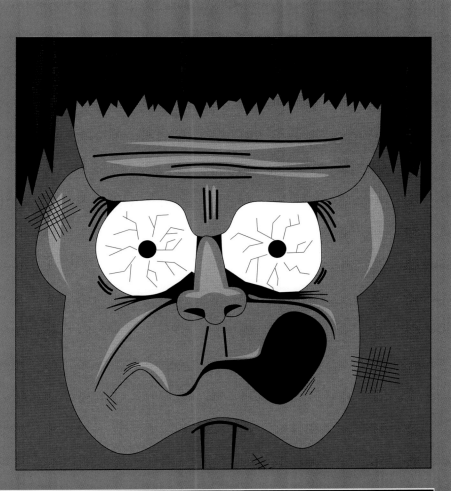

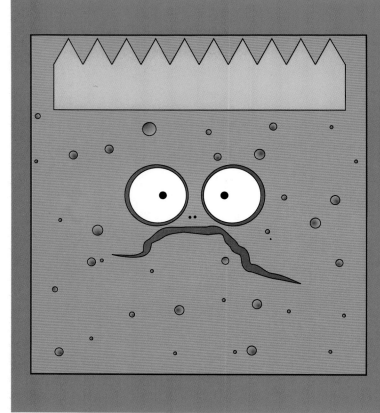

TOAD PRINCE

Pictured on page 15

Acrylic Paints:
   Black, bright lime green, dk. green, lt. apple
   green, metallic gold, bright red, white,
   and yellow-gold

Embellishment Materials:
   Craft glue
   Drawing paper

Painting:
Paint and detail pumpkin, referring to pattern.

Embellishing:
Cut a crown from drawing paper. Make sure
to allow enough length. Paint both sides with
metallic gold. Glue ends of crown together,
matching points on crown. Glue crown to top
of pumpkin.

GOOGLE-EYED GOURD

Pictured on page 15

Acrylic Paints:
   Black, lt. apple green, and very dk. sea foam green

Embellishment Materials:
   Glue gun and glue sticks
   Pipe cleaners, green: 2
   Styrofoam balls, 1½": 2
   Square of craft foam: dark sea foam green

Embellishing:
Insert pipe cleaners in top of gourd. Insert the other
end of pipe cleaners into styrofoam balls for eyes.
Position pipe cleaners, referring to photo. Enlarge
patterns as desired and cut nose, hands, and feet
from craft foam. Hot-glue in place, referring to photo
for placement. Pinch nose to shape it.

Painting:
Paint eyes on styrofoam balls, then paint and detail
gourd, referring to pattern.

SIDE-VIEW WITCH

Pictured on page 16

Acrylic Paints:
  Black, apple green,
  lt. sea foam green, tan,
  and off-white

Embellishment Materials:
  Glue gun and glue sticks
  Curly yarn, black
  Witch hat

Painting:
Paint and detail pumpkin,
referring to pattern.

Embellishing:
Cut yarn in varying lengths
and hot-glue it to top of
pumpkin for hair. Hot-glue
witch hat to top of pumpkin.

WRAPPED MUMMY

Pictured on page 16

Acrylic Paints:
  Black, red, and white

Embellishment Materials:
  Glue gun and glue sticks
  Fabric strips, cotton: white

Painting:
Paint and detail pumpkin,
referring to pattern.

Embellishing:
Wrap fabric strips around
pumpkin, mummy-style. Hot-
glue ends to fabric or pumpkin
wherever fabric strips end.

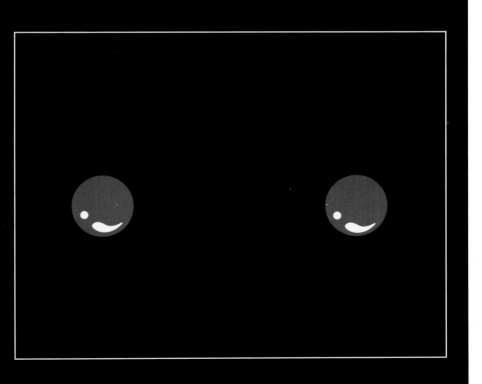

LITTLE DEVIL

Pictured on page 16

Acrylic Paints:
Black,
brick red,
orange-red,
and white

Painting:
Paint pumpkin,
referring
to pattern.

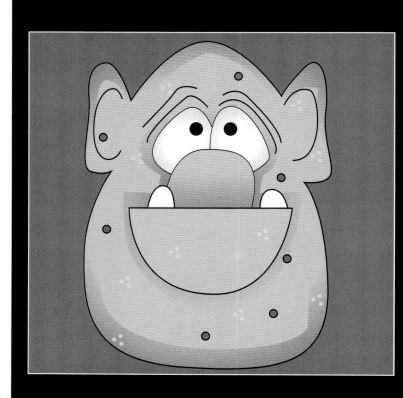

FUZZY FRANKENSTEIN

Pictured on page 16

Acrylic Paints:
Black, pastel blue, lt. green,
lt. lime green, white, and
bright yellow

Embellishment Materials:
Glue gun and glue sticks
Fake fur, yellow

Painting:
Paint and detail pumpkin, referring
to pattern.

Embellishing:
Hot-glue fake fur to top of pumpkin
for hair.

WEREWOLF

Pictured on page 17

Acrylic Paints:
Black, terra cotta brown, gray, taupe, lt. taupe, and white

Embellishment Materials:
Glue gun and glue sticks
Felt fabric, 2" triangles: brown (2)

Painting:
Paint and detail pumpkin, referring to pattern.

Embellishing:
Carefully remove stem from top of pumpkin. Hot-glue felt fabric triangles to top of pumpkin for ears, referring to photo for placement.

FIRE FACE

Pictured on page 18

Acrylic Paints:
Black, bright blue, dk. blue, pastel blue, sky blue, cream, orange, orchid, plum, red, and yellow

Painting:
Paint and detail pumpkin, referring to pattern. Do not base-coat pumpkin — begin by painting eyebrows, blending red into orange and orange into yellow to give the effect of fire. Paint remaining features. Last, paint unpainted areas of pumpkin with dk. blue.

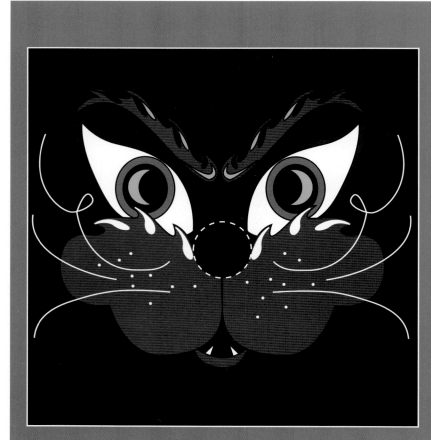

NINE LIVES

Pictured on page 19

Pumpkin must have a stem!

Acrylic Paints:
    Black, gray, dk. green, dk. rose, white, and yellow-gold

Embellishment Materials:
    Glue gun and glue sticks
    Felt fabric,
        2" triangles: black (2)

Painting:
Paint and detail pumpkin, referring to pattern. Paint pumpkin stem black for nose.

Embellishing:
Hot-glue felt fabric triangles to top of pumpkin for ears, referring to photo for placement.

ALL PUCKERED UP

Pictured on page 20

Pumpkin must have a stem!

Acrylic Paints:
    Black, dk. brown, gray, green, dk. green, dk. rose, lt. rose, and white

Embellishment Materials:
    Glue gun and glue sticks
    Witch hat
    Silk flowers, large: 3 or 4

Painting:
Paint and detail pumpkin, referring to pattern. Sponge pumpkin stem with dk. green for nose.

Embellishing:
Hot-glue silk flowers to witch hat, as desired. Hot-glue witch hat at an angle to top of pumpkin.

SKELETON SKULL

Pictured on page 21

Acrylic Paints:
Black and white

Painting:
Paint and detail pumpkin, referring to pattern.

ANGRY MUMMY

Pictured on page 21

Acrylic Paints:
Black,
lt. gray,
very lt. gray,
red, and white

Painting:
Paint and detail pumpkin, referring to pattern.

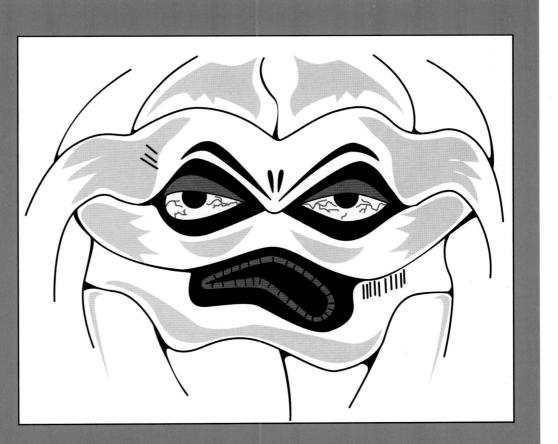

WART WITCH

Pictured on page 21

Acrylic Paints:
Black, coral, lime green, off-white, peach, bright red, and white

Embellishment Materials:
Craft glue
Plastic rhinestones: green (2)
Crinkled paper grass: green

Painting:
Paint and detail pumpkin, referring to pattern.

Embellishing:
Glue plastic rhinestones to front of pumpkin for eyes, referring to pattern for placement. Glue paper grass to top of pumpkin near and around stem for hair.

JAWS

Pictured on page 21

Acrylic Paints:
Black, dk. peach, very lt. peach, purple, red, and white

Embellishment Materials:
Glue gun and glue sticks
Square of craft foam: purple

Painting:
Paint and detail pumpkin, referring to pattern.

Embellishing:
Enlarge patterns as desired and cut fins and tail from craft foam. Hot-glue in place, referring to photo for placement.

BEACH BUM

Pictured on page 22

Acrylic Paints:
Black, baby blue,
dk. blue-gray,
red, and white

Embellishment Materials:
Glue gun and glue sticks
Plastic sun visor

Painting:
Paint and detail pumpkin,
referring to pattern.

Embellishing:
Hot-glue sides of sun visor to
top of pumpkin, referring to
photo for placement.

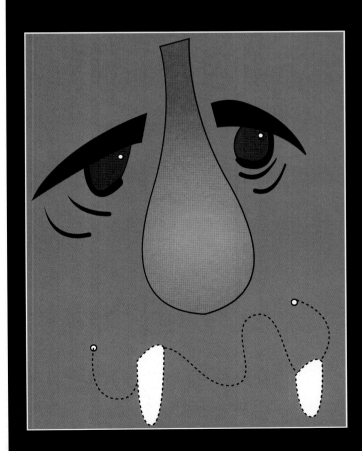

BAD HAIR DAY

Pictured on page 23

Acrylic Paints:
Black, gray, lt. gray, dk. olive green,
very lt. olive green, brick red, and white

Embellishment Materials:
Wire, 16-gauge: 2½ yds.
Wire cutters
Sculpting clay, white: 1 pkg.

Painting:
Paint and detail pumpkin, referring to pattern.

Embellishing:
Cut an 8" piece of wire. Twist to form mouth
and push sides into pumpkin. Form two
pointed teeth from sculpting clay around the
wire. Bake according to manufacturer's
directions. When cool, dry-brush teeth with
gray and lt. gray. Cut seven more pieces of
wire in different lengths. Twist and push into
top of pumpkin for hair.

WISE OLD OWL

Pictured on page 24

Acrylic Paints:

Black, dk. brown, lt. cocoa brown, dk. gold, lt. gold, gray, very lt. gray, lt. tan, white, and yellow-gold

Painting:

Paint and detail pumpkin, referring to pattern. Use an outward flipping motion to create feathers.

SPIDER FAMILY

Pictured on page 25

Acrylic Paints:
    Black and white

Embellishment Materials:
    Glue gun and glue sticks
    Paper twist, black:
        5 ft. for small spider / 10 ft. for large spider
    Wire, 24-gauge:
        7 ft. for small spider / 12 ft. for large spider

Painting:
Paint and detail pumpkins, referring to pattern.

Embellishing:
Cut eight 6" pieces of paper twist and eight 7" pieces of wire for small spider legs. Cut eight 15" pieces of paper twist and eight 17" pieces of wire for large spider legs. Untwist paper twist and scrunch it around the wires, leaving excess wire extending from one end of each wire. Secure ends of paper twist around wires with hot glue. Hot-glue at several places along edges. Push wire end of each leg into the top sides of pumpkin — four on each side. Bend and shape legs, as desired.

WEB OF LIFE

Pictured on page 25

Acrylic Paint:
    Black

Embellishment Materials:
    Craft glue
    Black spider, 5"
    Prepainted bugs, small: 1 pkg.
    Wire, 16-gauge: 1/2 yd.

Painting:
Paint and detail pumpkin, referring to pattern.

Embellishing:
Bend wire, as desired, and push it into top of black spider. Glue in place. Push other end of wire into top of pumpkin. Glue bugs on spider web.

BROOM HILDA

Pictured on page 25

Acrylic Paints:
    Black, dk. brown, dk. green, olive green,
    very lt. olive green, gold, plum, rose, and white

Embellishment Materials:
    Fabric, bright green: 1 yd.
    Stringed sequins, green: 5 yds.
    Witch hat
    Thread, black

Painting:
Paint and detail pumpkin, referring to pattern.

Embellishing:
Measure around opening of witch hat. Cut a 2"-wide strip of fabric that length. Cut remaining fabric in 1"- to 1¹/₂"-wide strips in uneven lengths. Lay these strips on top of 2"-wide strip and sew on. Mix in strips of sequins and sew on. Hand-sew 2"-wide strip to inside edge of witch hat. Put hat on top of pumpkin and trim fabric bangs.

MATILDA

Pictured on page 25

Acrylic Paints:
    Black, dk. sky blue, very lt. cranberry,
    fuschia, mauve, peach, and white

Embellishment Materials:
    Glue gun and glue sticks
    Curly doll hair, brunette
    Witch hat

Painting:
Paint and detail pumpkin, referring to pattern.

Embellishing:
Hot-glue doll hair to top of pumpkin. Hot-glue witch hat on top of pumpkin over doll hair.

SIMPLE SUNFLOWER & BEARY-SCARY BEAR

Pictured on page 26

Acrylic Paints:
Black, brown, gray, green, apple green, lt. khaki green, white, and yellow-gold

Embellishment Materials:
Ribbon(s)

Painting:
Paint and detail pumpkins, referring to patterns.

Embellishing:
Tie a ribbon(s) around stem of pumpkin.

HAT-SOME TRIO

Pictured on page 27

Acrylic Paints:
Black, dk. mauve, and white

Embellishment Materials:
Glue gun and glue sticks
Straw hats: 3
Ribbon bows: 3
Spanish moss
Silk or plastic greenery with berries
Feathers

Painting:
Paint and detail pumpkins, referring to patterns.

Embellishing:
Hot-glue a straw hat to the top of each pump-kin. Add Spanish moss, greenery, and feathers. Hot-glue a bow to each straw hat, as desired.

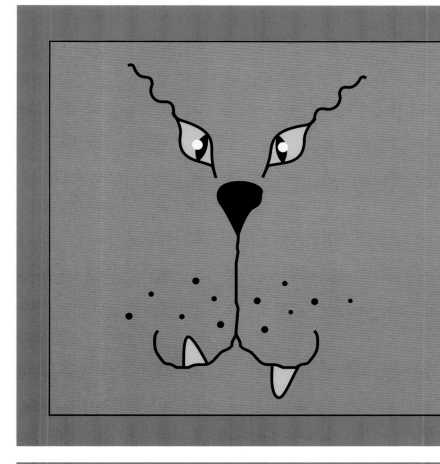

ALLEY CAT

Pictured on page 28

Acrylic Paints:
Black, lt. blue-gray, white, and yellow-gold

Embellishment Materials:
Wire, 16-gauge
Wire cutters

Painting:
Paint and detail pumpkin, referring to pattern.

Embellishing:
Cut six 6" pieces of wire. Curl wire to form whiskers. Push three into each side of pumpkin. Carefully remove stem from top of pumpkin. Make ears by referring to instructions on page 12 for making ears out of wire.

SCAR FACE

Pictured on page 28

Acrylic Paints:
Black,
lt. blue-gray,
olive green,
and white

Painting:
Paint and detail pumpkin, referring to pattern. To get paint to "drip," dilute it to the consistency of watercolor paint. Allow paint to drip down pumpkin, referring to photo.

GRIM REAPER

Pictured on page 28

Acrylic Paints:
Black and orange

Painting:
Paint and detail pumpkin, referring to pattern. Base-coat entire pumpkin with black. When dry, paint the grim reaper with orange. Apply as many coats of orange as necessary to completely cover the black base coat.

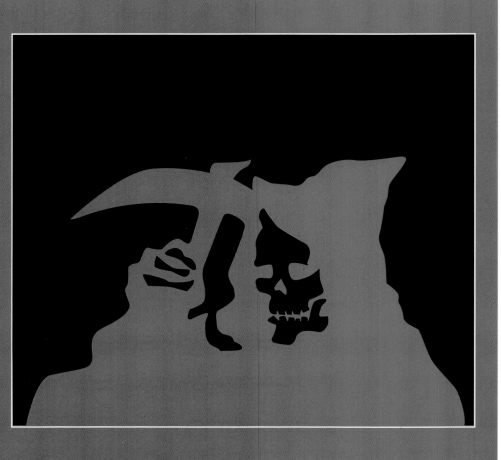

CRESCENT MOON

Pictured on page 28

Acrylic Paints:
Lt. turquoise

Painting:
Paint pumpkin, referring to pattern. The actual pattern will not be painted, but rather the remaining surface of the pumpkin. This creates a silhouette effect.

BARNYARD FRIENDS

Pictured on page 29

Acrylic Paints:
Black, baby blue, gray, silver gray, peach, pink, very lt. pink, white, and pastel yellow

Materials to Assemble Stand:
Plywood block, 11" x 11" x $^3/_4$"
Allthread, $^3/_8$": 36"
Nuts, $^3/_8$": 2
Washer, $^3/_8$"
Drill and drill bits, $^3/_4$" and $^3/_8$"

Painting:
Paint and detail pumpkins, referring to patterns. Paint plywood block with dark green.

Helpful Hints:
When planning a series of stacking pumpkins, it is always best to choose pumpkins that have a flat bottom, and as flat a top as possible. Carefully remove stems from tops of all pumpkins, except for the smallest (top) pumpkin, if a stem is desired.

Assembling Stand:

When paint is dry, drill a $^3/_4$" hole in center bottom of plywood block $^3/_8$" deep. Drill a $^3/_8$" hole in center of $^3/_4$" hole. Screw a nut onto the allthread, $^3/_4$" from bottom. Place washer over nut and place allthread through $^3/_8$" hole, from top of plywood block. Screw remaining nut onto allthread from bottom. When pumpkins have been painted and sealed, stack from largest to smallest. Begin by drilling a hole in the tops and bottoms of each pumpkin. Let the pumpkins sit for a few minutes for any liquid to drain. Carefully stack them onto the allthread. A folded napkin or paper towel can be placed around the allthread between each pumpkin to absorb the liquid that will continue to drain from each pumpkin.

CIRCUS CLOWN

Pictured on page 30

Acrylic Paints:

Black, blue, plum, red, white, and yellow-gold

Embellishment Materials:

Glue gun and glue sticks

Wood glue

Felt top hat, 3" high

Wooden knob, 1½"

Wooden dowel, ³⁄₁₆": 3" length

Curling ribbon: orange, purple, red, and yellow

Silk flower, large: bright blue

Painting:

Paint and detail pumpkin, referring to pattern.

Paint wooden knob with red.

Embellishing:

Sharpen one end of wooden dowel with a pencil sharpener. Glue flat end of dowel into wooden knob with wood glue. Push sharpened end of dowel into front of pumpkin for nose. Curl curling ribbon and hot-glue to top of pumpkin for hair. Hot-glue top hat in place and hot-glue silk flower to side of hat.

SPARKLE-EYES

Pictured on page 30

Acrylic Paints:

Black, dk. mauve, and white

Embellishment Materials:

Glue gun and glue sticks

Dried leaves and weeds

Plaid ribbon, 1½" wide

Painting:

Paint and detail pumpkin, referring to pattern.

Embellishing:

Tie a bow from the plaid ribbon. Hot-glue dried leaves and weeds to top of pumpkin. Carefully hot-glue bow on top of dried arrangement, as desired.

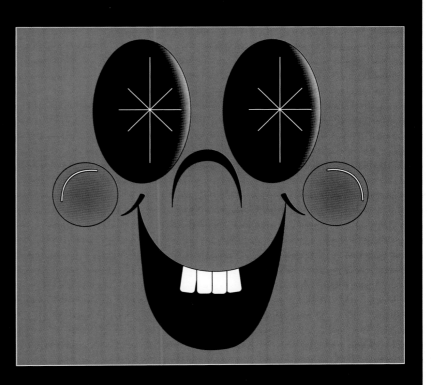

OH MY GOSH!

Pictured on page 30

Acrylic Paints:
Black, bright green, and white

Painting:
Paint and detail pumpkin, referring to pattern.

FOREVER FRIENDS

Pictured on page 30

Acrylic Paints:
Black, dk. blue-gray, very lt. gray, green, dk. lavender, orange, pink, bright red, white, and yellow

Painting:
Paint and detail pumpkin, referring to patterns.

HAUNTED HOUSE

Pictured on page 31

Acrylic Paints:
Black, bright green, hot pink, plum, white, and yellow

Painting:
Paint and detail pumpkin, referring to pattern.

BOUNTIFUL HARVEST

Pictured on page 32

Acrylic Paints:

Black, lt. brown, green, dk. green, lt. apple green, olive green, dk. melon, peach, red, terra cotta brown, and yellow-gold

Painting:

Paint and detail pumpkins, referring to patterns.

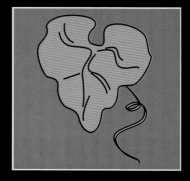
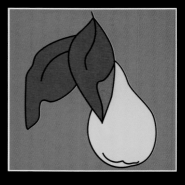
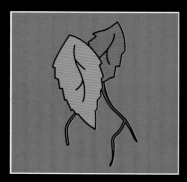
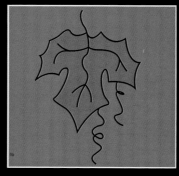
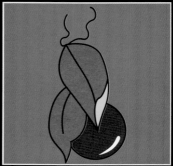
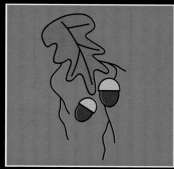

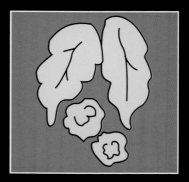
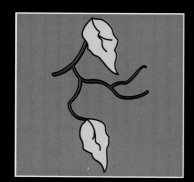

GARGOYLE

Pictured on page 33

Acrylic Paint:
Black

Painting:
Paint and detail pumpkin, referring to pattern.

PIRATE

Pictured on page 33

Acrylic Paints:
Black, cocoa brown, very lt. cocoa brown, off-white, and red

Embellishment Materials:
Silk scarf
Hoop post earring, gold: large

Painting:
Paint and detail pumpkin, referring to pattern.

Embellishing:
Tie the scarf around the pumpkin, off to one side. Push post earring into one side of pumpkin, opposite from scarf.

DEVIL

Pictured on page 33

Acrylic Paints:
   Black, cantaloupe, red, white, and yellow-gold

Embellishment Materials:
   Glue gun and glue sticks
   Felt fabric, red
   Wire, 16-gauge
   Wire cutters

Painting:
Paint and detail pumpkin, referring to pattern.

Embellishing:
Make horns by referring to instructions on page 12 for making ears out of wire and covering them with fabric. Highlight horns with acrylic paints.

FANCY FACE

Pictured on page 33

Acrylic Paints:
   Black, copper, and white

Embellishment Materials:
   Glue gun and glue sticks
   Small plastic pumpkins: 2
   Curling ribbon: black, orange
   Pumpkin garland

Painting:
Paint and detail pumpkin, referring to pattern.

Embellishing:
Hot-glue plastic pumpkins in eyes. Curl curling ribbon and hot-glue to top of pumpkin. Cut pumpkin garland into various lengths and hot-glue, intertwined with curling ribbon.

FLAVORFUL TURKEY

Pictured on page 34

Acrylic Paints:
Black, dk. green, burnt orange, dk. rose, tan, white, and yellow-gold

Embellishment Materials:
Suckers:
Green, 2
Orange, 3
Purple, 2
Red, 1
Yellow, 4

Painting:
Paint and detail pumpkin, referring to pattern.

Embellishing:
Push sucker sticks into pumpkin at dots shown on pattern.

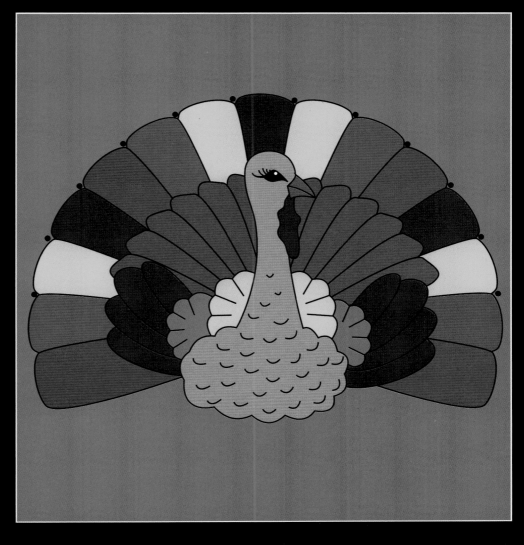

SO SURPRISED

Pictured on page 36

Acrylic Paints:
Black and white

Embellishment Materials:
Ribbon(s)

Painting:
Paint and detail pumpkin, referring to pattern.

Embellishing:
Tie a ribbon(s) around stem of pumpkin.

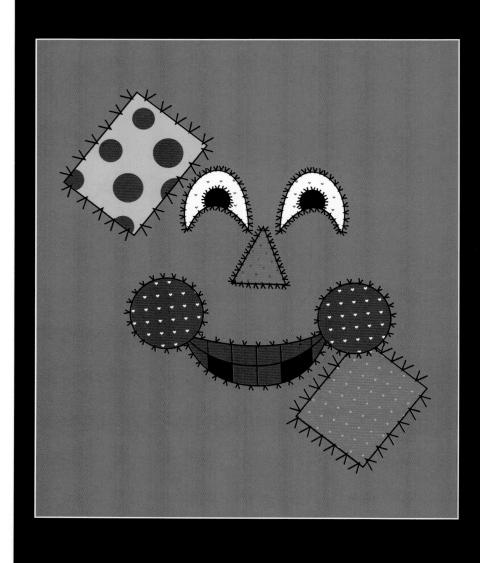

PATCHWORK
SCARECROW

**Pictured on
page 35**

Acrylic Paints:
  Black, blue, cranberry,
  green, white, and
  yellow-gold

**Embellishment
Materials:**
  Glue gun and glue sticks
  Straw hat
  Straw

Painting:
Paint and detail pumpkin,
referring to pattern.

Embellishing:
Hot-glue straw to top of
pumpkin for hair. Hot-glue
straw hat on top of pump-
kin over straw hair.

LITTLE
VAMPIRE

Pictured on page 36

Acrylic Paints:
  Black and white

Painting:
Paint and detail pumpkin,
referring to pattern.

BOOK WORM

Pictured on page 37

Acrylic Paints:
   Black, bright blue, metallic gold, and white

Embellishment Materials:
   Wire, 16-gauge: 48"
   Wire cutters
   Small wooden bead, lime green

Painting:
Base-coat largest pumpkin with bright blue and remaining pumpkins with white. Sponge-paint all pumpkins (except head) with bright blue. Eyes (and mouth) should be painted on pumpkin after eye glasses have been positioned.

Embellishing:
Cut two 12" pieces of wire. Twist to form antennae. Push into top of pumpkin. Paint antennae metallic gold with black ends. Use remaining 24" of wire to form eye glasses. Push ends of wire glasses into sides of pumpkin and paint metallic gold. Line pumpkins up in a row from largest to smallest to form a "worm."

GOBBLING GOURD

Pictured on page 37

Acrylic Paints:
   Black and white

Embellishment Materials:
   Glue gun and glue sticks
   Colored feathers: 10" (6), 5" (12)
   Chenille bumps: red (2), orange (6)
   Square of craft foam: peach

Painting:
Paint and detail gourd, referring to pattern.

Embellishing:
Enlarge patterns as desired and cut beak (top and bottom) from craft foam. Hot-glue in place, referring to photo for placement. Hot-glue red chenille bumps on top of top beak for waddle. Hot-glue three short feathers on each side of gourd for wings and remaining six short feathers at back of gourd for tail. Hot-glue long feathers over short feathers at tail. Cut orange chenille bumps apart and hot-glue three on each side for feet. Shape to resemble bird feet.

SAM SCARECROW

Pictured on page 37

Acrylic Paints:
Black, brown, blue-gray, caucasian fleshtone, lt. rose, rust, lt. shade of rust, and off-white

Embellishment Materials:
Glue gun and glue sticks
Stuffed scarecrow

Painting:
Paint and detail pumpkin, referring to pattern.

Embellishing:
Remove scarecrow's head from stuffed body. Hot-glue pumpkin into its place.

PLAID PUMPKIN

Pictured on page 38

Acrylic Paints:
Olive green, orange, rust, and lt. rust

Embellishment Materials:
Glue gun and glue sticks
Wired silk leaves and vines

Painting:
Paint pumpkin, referring to pattern.

Embellishing:
Hot-glue silk leaves and vines to top of pumpkin, as desired.

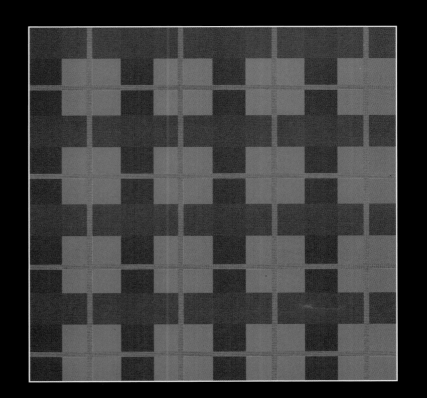

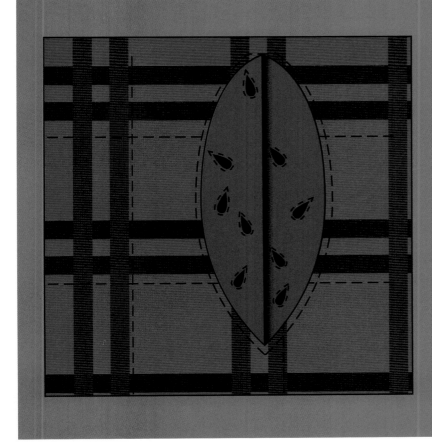

WATERMELON

Pictured on page 38

Acrylic Paints:
Black, dk. green, olive green, dk. olive green, and red

Embellishment Materials:
Glue gun and glue sticks
Wired silk leaves and vines

Painting:
Paint and detail pumpkin, referring to pattern.

Embellishing:
Hot-glue silk leaves and vines to top of pumpkin, as desired.

SUNFLOWER

Pictured on page 38

Acrylic Paints:
Black, brown, brown-gray, terra cotta brown, lt. gold, burnt orange, and white

Embellishment Materials:
Glue gun and glue sticks
Wired silk leaves and vines
Water-base stain

Painting:
Paint pumpkin, referring to pattern.

Embellishing:
Stain with water-base stain. Allow to dry thoroughly. Hot-glue silk leaves and vines to top of pumpkin, as desired.

WINTER CARDINAL

Pictured on page 39

Acrylic Paints:
Black, cocoa brown, lt. cocoa brown, very dk. brown, cranberry, very lt. cranberry, fuschia, gold, dk. green, moss green, sea foam green, and off-white

Embellishment Materials:
Glue gun and glue sticks
Pine sprays with holly berries
Pinecones
Cardinal figure

Painting:
Paint and detail pumpkin, referring to pattern.

Embellishing:
Hot-glue pine sprays, pinecones, and cardinal to top of pumpkin.

COUNTRY ROAD

Pictured on page 39

Acrylic Paints:
Black, very dk. brown, cocoa brown, lt. cocoa brown, cranberry, very lt. cranberry, fuschia, gold, dk. green, moss green, sea foam green, off-white, purple, and dk. purple

Embellishment Materials:
Glue gun and glue sticks
Silk fall leaves
Scarecrow figure

Painting:
Paint and detail pumpkin, referring to pattern.

Embellishing:
Hot-glue silk leaves and scarecrow to top of pumpkin.

BERRIES

Pictured on page 39

Acrylic Paints:
Black, copper, blue-gray, very dk. gray, lt. olive green, brick red, lt. turquoise, and off-white

Embellishment Materials:
Glue gun and glue sticks
Silk fall leaves
Plastic grapes

Painting:
Paint pumpkin, referring to pattern.

Embellishing:
Hot-glue silk leaves and plastic grapes to top of pumpkin.

PATCHWORK PUMPKIN

Pictured on page 40

Acrylic Paints:

Black, blue, lt. burgundy, gray, dk. green, dk. sea foam green, orange, purple, white, and yellow

Embellishment Materials:

Glue gun and glue sticks
Craft glue
Doily, ecru: 8"
Measuring tape, yellow
Pin cushion, red
Wooden thread spools:
    2½" (1), 1⅛" (5), ¾" (3)
Thimbles, silver: 2
Brass scissors charm, 2½"
Embroidery floss
    in assorted colors
Buttons, assortment
Pins, assortment
Plastic mice:
    1½" (2)
Antiquing gel, brown
Gloss spray sealer

Painting:

Paint and detail pumpkin, referring to pattern.

Embellishing:

Carefully remove stem from top of pumpkin. Apply a thin layer of craft glue to back of doily. Centering, press on top of pumpkin. Allow to dry thoroughly. Antique tape measure, thread spools, thimbles, and scissors charm with antiquing gel. Allow to dry thoroughly. Tie a loopy bow in center of tape measure leaving two 25" tails. Wrap thread spools with assorted colors of embroidery floss leaving 5" to 6" tails. Hot-glue largest spool, pin cushion, and tape measure bow to top of doily, referring to photo for placement. Stack and hot-glue on remaining thread spools, thimbles, buttons, scissors charm, and mice. Loop thread and bow tails and secure with hot glue. Stick pins in pin cushion and in thread spools, as desired.

NICE DOGGY

Pictured on page 41

Acrylic Paints:
 Black, dk. gold, olive green, dk. peach, bright red, and off-white

Embellishment Materials:
 Glue gun and glue sticks
 Felt fabric, mustard
 Wire, 16-gauge: gold
 Wire cutters

Painting:
Paint and detail pumpkin, referring to pattern.

Embellishing:
Cut six 6" pieces of wire. Curl wire to form whiskers. Push three into each side of pumpkin. Make ears by referring to instructions on page 12 for making ears out of wire and covering them with fabric. Highlight ears with acrylic paints.

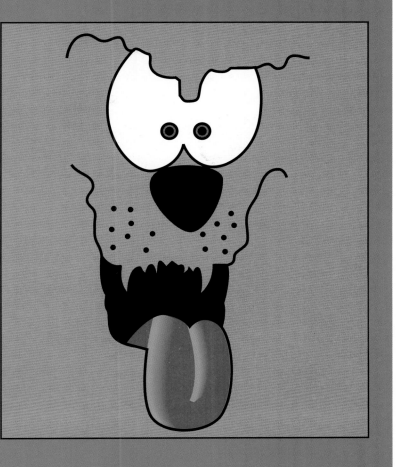

COUNTRY CROW

Pictured on page 41

Acrylic Paints:
 Black, mustard, rust, dk. taupe, and white

Embellishment Materials:
 Glue gun and glue sticks
 Straw hat, 6" diameter

Painting:
Paint and detail pumpkin, referring to pattern.

Embellishing:
Hot-glue straw hat to top of pumpkin.

BEARY SPECIAL BEAR

Pictured on page 41

Acrylic Paints:
Black, very lt. mauve, lt. tan, dk. taupe, and white

Embellishment Materials:
Glue gun and glue sticks
Strip of blue-print cotton fabric

Painting:
Paint and detail pumpkin, referring to pattern.

Embellishing:
Tie fabric strip into a bow with long tails. Hot-glue bow to top of pumpkin and tails to sides of pumpkin for a hair bow.

FRIGHTENED CAT

Pictured on page 41

Acrylic Paints:
Black, copper, and dk. gold

Embellishment Materials:
Glue gun and glue sticks
Wired silk leaves

Painting:
Paint and detail pumpkin, referring to pattern.

Embellishing:
Hot-glue silk leaves to top of pumpkin.

JACK-O-RABBIT

Pictured on page 42

Acrylic Paints:
Black, lt. brown, lt. gray, green, lt. green, pink, lt. tan, very dk. taupe, and off-white

Embellishment Materials:
Glue gun and glue sticks
Wire, 20-gauge: 1 yd.
Wire cutters
Craft foam: gray

Painting:
Paint and detail pumpkin, referring to pattern. Paint highlights on rabbit ears.

Embellishing:
Enlarge patterns as desired and cut ears from craft foam. Cut two 8" pieces of wire. Hot-glue wire along center back of each ear leaving at least 1" extending at lower ends. Press ears together at the bottom, around wire, to form a tuck in craft foam. Push wires into top of pumpkin and bend ears, as desired. Cut four more pieces of wire in 5" lengths. Twist and push into front of pumpkin for whiskers.

HAPPY HOBOS

Pictured on page 43

Acrylic Paints:
Black, gray, red, light rust, and white

Embellishment Materials:
Glue gun and glue sticks
Assorted hats: 3
Silk scarf

Painting:
Paint and detail pumpkins, referring to patterns.

Embellishing:
Tie silk scarf into a bow. Hot-glue scarf and hats onto tops of pumpkins.

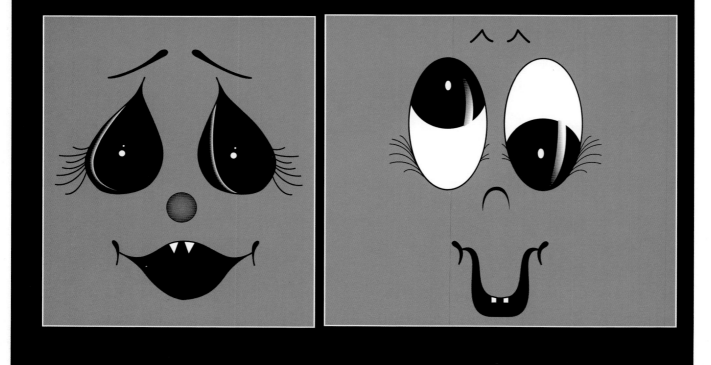

MOON EYES

Pictured on page 44

Acrylic Paints:
Black,
dk. blue-gray,
navy blue,
dk. gold,
yellow-gold, and
sparkle glaze

Painting:
Paint and detail
pumpkin, referring
to pattern. Paint
over eyes with
sparkle glaze.

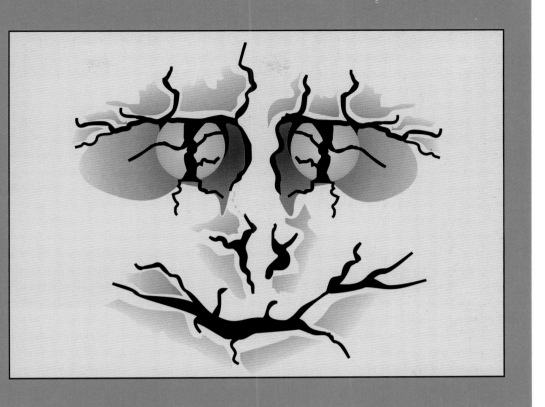

FULL MOON

Pictured on page 44

Acrylic Paints:
Black and
bright yellow

Painting:
Paint and detail
pumpkin, referring
to pattern.

PUMPKIN COACH

Pictured on page 45

Acrylic Paints:

    Black, metallic gold,
    silver-gray, and white

Materials to Assemble Stand:

    Wooden plaque, oval: $6^5/_8$" x 5"
    Wooden spoked wheels: $2^1/_2$" (4)
    Wooden pegs for axles: 2" (4)
    Drill and drill bit, $5/_{16}$"
    Wood glue
    Gloss spray sealer

Painting:

Paint and detail pumpkin, referring to pattern. Paint oval plaque and center and outer areas of wheels with white. Paint spokes, pegs, and routed edge of oval plaque with metallic gold. Spray with spray sealer.

Assembling Stand:

Refer to photo to mark placement for wheels on oval plaque. Drill holes. Slide one peg through each wheel and glue into drilled holes. Allow to dry thoroughly.

FAT LADY

Pictured on page 46

Acrylic Paints:
Black, robin egg blue, lt. robin egg blue, teal green, lt. teal green, peach, lt. pink, red, and white

Embellishment Materials:
Curly wig, white
Hoop post earrings, large
Straight pins

Painting:
Paint and detail pumpkin, referring to pattern.

Embellishing:
Pin wig to top of pumpkin. Push post earrings into sides of pumpkin.

MAD SCIENTIST

Pictured on page 46

Acrylic Paints:
Black, cranberry, very lt. gold, bright green, very lt. peach, and white

Embellishment Materials:
Wiglets, white: 2
Straight pins

Painting:
Paint and detail pumpkin, referring to pattern.

Embellishing:
Pin wig to sides of pumpkin.

BRIDE OF FRANKENSTEIN

Pictured on page 46

Acrylic Paints:
Black, cranberry, gray, dk. green, lt. shade of dk. green, and white

Embellishment Materials:
Glue gun and glue sticks
Stuffing, polyester
Spray paint, black

Painting:
Paint and detail pumpkin, referring to pattern.
Sponge paint background.
Spray paint polyester stuffing.

Embellishing:
Hot-glue stuffing to top of pumpkin.

TONGUE-LASHING CLOWN

Pictured on page 46

Acrylic Paints:
Black, bone, dk. orchid, and purple

Embellishment Materials:
Clown wig, multi-colored
Straight pins

Painting:
Paint and detail pumpkin, referring to pattern.
Sponge paint background.

Embellishing:
Pin wig to top of pumpkin.

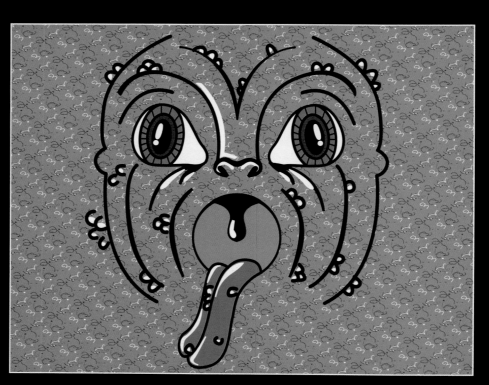

INSECT

Pictured on page 47

Acrylic Paints:
Black, very dk. brown, bright lime green, very dk. brown, very dk. sea foam green, and very dk. taupe

Embellishment Materials:
Glue gun and glue sticks
Wire, 16-gauge: 24"
Wire cutters
Small wooden beads, green: 2

Painting:
Paint and detail pumpkin, referring to pattern.

Embellishing:
Cut two 12" pieces of wire. Curl wire to form antennae. Hot-glue a bead to the end of each antennae. Push the antennae into top of pumpkin and position, as desired.

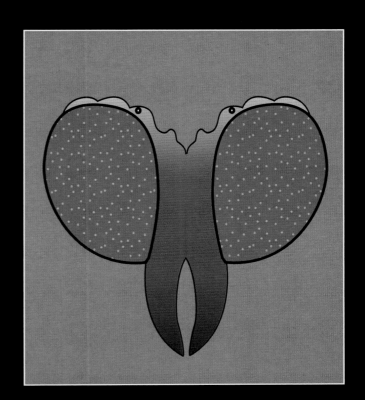

ALIEN

Pictured on page 47

Acrylic Paints:
Black, very lt. gold, lt. gray, olive green, lt. teal green, very lt. mustard, and dk. brick red

Embellishment Materials:
Pipe cleaners, white: 2
Styrofoam balls, 1¹/₂": 2

Painting:
Paint and detail pumpkins, referring to patterns. Paint styrofoam balls.

Embellishing:
Push a styrofoam ball into the end of each pipe cleaner for antennae. Push the opposite end of each pipe cleaner into top of pumpkin and position, as desired.

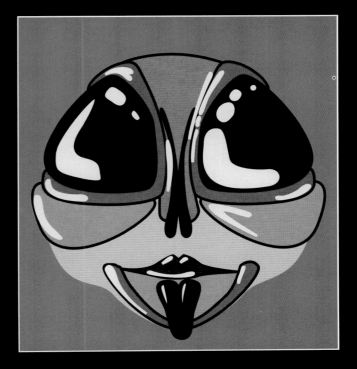

MINI PUMPKINS

Pictured on page 48

Acrylic Paints:

Black, dk. gray, bright green, orange, dk. orchid, orange-red, white, and yellow-gold

Painting:

Paint and detail pumpkins, referring to patterns.

PUMPKIN TOPIARY TREE

Pictured on page 49

Acrylic Paints:

Dk. brown, gold, and orange

Materials to Assemble Tree:

Papier-mâché pumpkin,
    4¹/₂" diameter
Silk leaf vine
Wooden dowel,
    11" long x ³/₄" diameter
Clay pot, 6" diameter
Floral tape, brown
Craft knife
Glue gun and glue sticks
Sculpting clay
Plaster of Paris
Florist's foam
Spanish moss
Flower picks in fall colors

Painting and Assembling:

Paint clay pot with dk. brown and wrap dowel with brown floral tape. Make a hole in bottom of pumpkin with craft knife. Push dowel into hole and hot-glue in place. Seal hole in bottom of clay pot with small piece of sculpting clay. Mix plaster according to manufacturer's directions and pour into clay pot. (If the clay pot was completely filled with plaster all at once, the pot would break because of the heat of the plaster.) Place dowel in clay pot, centering, and secure so it cannot shift. Allow to set up. Continue process until clay pot is full, leaving enough room to add florist's foam. Dry-brush grooves in pumpkin and wrapped dowel with dk. brown. Dry-brush both sides of vine with dk. brown, gold, and orange. Poke holes in top of pumpkin and insert vines and hot-glue in place. Add florist's foam to inside top of clay pot and cover with Spanish moss. Add flower picks that coordinate with fall colors.

MINIATURE PUMPKINS

Pictured on page 49

Acrylic Paints:

Black, bright blue, brick red, and white

Painting:

Paint and detail pumpkins, referring to patterns.

TOLE PUMPKIN

Pictured on page 50

Acrylic Paints:
Black, bright green, peach, rose, and white

Building Materials, Tools & Embellishments:
Pine, ½" or ¾"
Saw
Sandpaper
Wood sealer
Wood glue
Wire, 16-gauge
Wire cutters
Curly doll hair, auburn

Preparing Wood:
Make a photo copy of pattern pieces provided, reducing or enlarging as desired. Trace pattern onto pine and cut out. Sand until rough edges are smooth. Seal wood with wood sealer according to manufacturer's directions. Allow to dry thoroughly. Place wood pieces together to make sure they fit nicely. Take pieces apart.

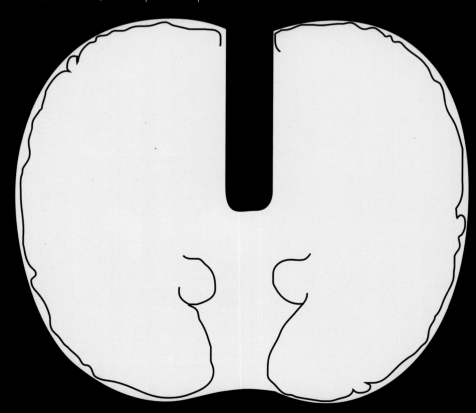

Painting:
Base-coat one side and all edges of each pumpkin piece with two to three coats of acrylic paint. Allow to dry thoroughly. Base-coat remaining side of pumpkin pieces with the same number of coats, and let dry. Paint and detail both sides, referring to patterns. When thoroughly dry, place pieces together and secure with a small amount of wood glue.

Embellishing:
Use wire to form eye glasses. Glue glasses to pumpkin's nose and glue doll hair to top of pumpkin.

METRIC CONVERSIONS

INCHES TO MILLIMETRES AND CENTIMETRES

MM-Millimetres   CM-Centimetres

INCHES	MM	CM	INCHES	CM	INCHES	CM
1/8	3	0.9	9	22.9	30	76.2
1/4	6	0.6	10	25.4	31	78.7
3/8	10	1.0	11	27.9	32	81.3
1/2	13	1.3	12	30.5	33	83.8
5/8	16	1.6	13	33.0	34	86.4
3/4	19	1.9	14	35.6	35	88.9
7/8	22	2.2	15	38.1	36	91.4
1	25	2.5	16	40.6	37	94.0
1 1/4	32	3.2	17	43.2	38	96.5
1 1/2	38	3.8	18	45.7	39	99.1
1 3/4	44	4.4	19	48.3	40	101.6
2	51	5.1	20	50.8	41	104.1
2 1/2	64	6.4	21	53.3	42	106.7
3	76	7.6	22	55.9	43	109.2
3 1/2	89	8.9	23	58.4	44	111.8
4	102	10.2	24	61.0	45	114.3
4 1/2	114	11.4	25	63.5	46	116.8
5	127	12.7	26	66.0	47	119.4
6	152	15.2	27	68.6	48	121.9
7	178	17.8	28	71.1	49	124.5
8	203	20.3	29	73.7	50	127.0

YARDS TO METRES

YARDS	METRES	YARDS	METRES	YARDS	METRES	YARDS	METRES	YARDS	METRES
1/8	0.11	2 1/8	1.94	4 1/8	3.77	6 1/8	5.60	8 1/8	7.43
1/4	0.23	2 1/4	2.06	4 1/4	3.89	6 1/4	5.72	8 1/4	7.54
3/8	0.34	2 3/8	2.17	4 3/8	4.00	6 3/8	5.83	8 3/8	7.66
1/2	0.46	2 1/2	2.29	4 1/2	4.11	6 1/2	5.94	8 1/2	7.77
5/8	0.57	2 5/8	2.40	4 5/8	4.23	6 5/8	6.06	8 5/8	7.89
3/4	0.69	2 3/4	2.51	4 3/4	4.34	6 3/4	6.17	8 3/4	8.00
7/8	0.80	2 7/8	2.63	4 7/8	4.46	6 7/8	6.29	8 7/8	8.12
1	0.91	3	2.74	5	4.57	7	6.40	9	8.23
1 1/8	1.03	3 1/8	2.86	5 1/8	4.69	7 1/8	6.52	9 1/8	8.34
1 1/4	1.14	3 1/4	2.97	5 1/4	4.80	7 1/4	6.63	9 1/4	8.46
1 3/8	1.26	3 3/8	3.09	5 3/8	4.91	7 3/8	6.74	9 3/8	8.57
1 1/2	1.37	3 1/2	3.20	5 1/2	5.03	7 1/2	6.86	9 1/2	8.69
1 5/8	1.49	3 5/8	3.31	5 5/8	5.14	7 5/8	6.97	9 5/8	8.80
1 3/4	1.60	3 3/4	3.43	5 3/4	5.26	7 3/4	7.09	9 3/4	8.92
1 7/8	1.71	3 7/8	3.54	5 7/8	5.37	7 7/8	7.20	9 7/8	9.03
2	1.83	4	3.66	6	5.49	8	7.32	10	9.14

INDEX